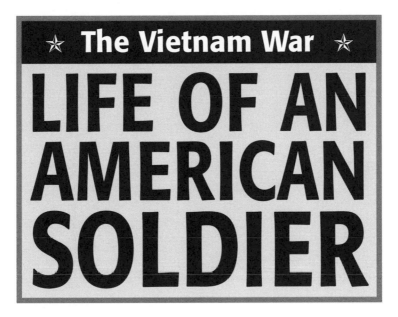

Titles in The American War Library series include:

World War II
Hitler and the Nazis
Kamikazes
Leaders and Generals
Life as a POW
Life of an American Soldier in
  Europe
Strategic Battles in Europe
Strategic Battles in the Pacific
The War at Home
Weapons of War

The Civil War
Leaders of the North and South
Life Among the Soldiers and
  Cavalry
Lincoln and the Abolition of
  Slavery

Strategic Battles
Weapons of War

The Persian Gulf
Leaders and Generals
Life of an American Soldier
The War Against Iraq
Weapons of War

The Vietnam War
A History of U.S. Involvement
The Home Front: Americans
  Protest the War
Leaders and Generals
Life of an American Soldier
Life as a POW
Weapons of War

AMERICAN
WAR LIBRARY
★ ★ ★ ★

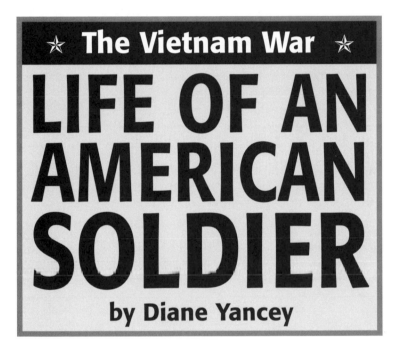

★ The Vietnam War ★

LIFE OF AN AMERICAN SOLDIER

by Diane Yancey

Lucent Books, P.O. Box 289011, San Diego, CA 92198-9011

Library of Congress Cataloging-in-Publication Data

Yancey, Diane.
    Life of an American Soldier / by Diane Yancey
        p.   cm.—(American war library. Vietnam War)
    Summary: Describes the men and women who fought in the
    Vietnam War, the kind of war they fought, and the distress and
    difficulty they suffered on their return to the United States.
    Includes bibliographical references and index.
        ISBN 1-56006-676-8 (lib. bdg. : alk. paper)
        1. Vietnamese Conflict, 1961–1975—United States—
    Juvenile literature. 2. Vietnamese Conflict, 1961–1975—
    Psychological aspects—Juvenile literature. 3. Soldiers—
    United States—Psychology—Juvenile literature. 4. United
    States. Army—Military life—Juvenile literature. [1. Vietnamese
    Conflict, 1961–1975. 2. Soldiers. 3. United States. Army—
    Military life.] I. Title. II. Series.
        DS558.Y36   2001
        959.704'3373—dc21   00-008386

★ Contents ★

A Nation Forged by War

The United States, like many nations, was forged and defined by war. Despite Benjamin Franklin's opinion that "There never was a good war or a bad peace," the United States owes its very existence to the War of Independence, one to which Franklin wholeheartedly subscribed. The country forged by war in 1776 was tempered and made stronger by the Civil War in the 1860s.

The Texas Revolution, the Mexican-American War, and the Spanish-American War expanded the country's borders and gave it overseas possessions. These wars made the United States a world power, but this status came with a price, as the nation became a key but reluctant player in both World War I and World War II.

Each successive war further defined the country's role on the world stage. Following World War II, U.S. foreign policy redefined itself to focus on the role of defender, not only of the freedom of its own citizens, but also of the freedom of people everywhere. During the cold war that followed World War II until the collapse of the Soviet Union, defending the world meant fighting communism. This goal, manifested in the Korean and Vietnam conflicts, proved elusive, and soured the American public on its achievability. As the United States emerged as the world's sole superpower, American foreign policy has been guided less by national interest and more on protecting international human rights. But as involvement in Somalia and Kosovo prove, this goal has been equally elusive.

As a result, the country's view of itself changed. Bolstered by victories in World Wars I and II, Americans first relished the role of protector. But, as war followed war in a seemingly endless procession, Americans began to doubt their leaders, their motives, and themselves. The Vietnam War especially caused people to question the validity of sending its young people to die in places where they were not particularly wanted and for people who did not seem especially grateful.

While the most obvious changes brought about by America's wars have been geopolitical in nature, many other aspects of society have been touched. War often does not bring about change directly, but acts instead like the catalyst in a chemical reaction, accelerating changes already in progress.

Some of these changes have been societal. The role of women in the United States had been slowly changing, but World War II put thousands into the workforce and into uniform. They might have gone back to being housewives after the war, but equality, once experienced, would not be forgotten.

Likewise, wars have accelerated technological change. The necessity for faster airplanes and a more destructive bomb led to the development of jet planes and nuclear energy. Artificial fibers developed for parachutes in the 1940s were used in the clothing of the 1950s.

Lucent Books' American War Library covers key wars in the development of the nation. Each war is covered in several volumes, to allow for more detail, context, and to provide volumes on often neglected subjects, such as the kamikazes of World War II, or weapons used in the Civil War. As with all Lucent Books, notes, annotated bibliographies, and appendixes such as glossaries give students a launching point for further research. In addition, sidebars and archival photographs enhance the text. Together, each volume in The American War Library will aid students in understanding how America's wars have shaped and changed its politics, economics, and society.

Impossible Mission

he war in Vietnam was the first "television war" in history, a struggle that millions of Americans watched every night on the evening news. The armed and camouflage-clad men who moved across their screens— young, nervous, uncertain in battle— were their sons and brothers, thousands of miles from home, fighting homesickness, fear, and ruthless adversaries. Sometimes the camera caught these men on the streets of cities like Saigon and Hue. More often, they were seen plodding through jungles and rice paddies, alert for booby traps and snipers that could kill or maim a person in the blink of an eye.

As bullets flew, they ducked and scrambled and fired on the enemy when they could find him. In quiet moments, they pondered whether the war was right or wrong. "After a few months, it began to seem crazy," William Ehrhart, a marine, observed. "Maybe we Americans weren't the guys in white hats, riding white horses.

Maybe we shouldn't be in Vietnam. Maybe I'd gotten my ass out in these bushes for nothing."[1]

A Long and Futile War

The first American soldiers who went to Vietnam were military advisors, sent into the region in the wake of World War II to help establish and strengthen a pro-American government. (The term "soldier" technically refers to troops in an army, but in this book it denotes all enlisted men including marines.) At stake, according to Presidents Truman, Eisenhower, Kennedy, and Johnson, was the security of the free world. If Communists succeeded in gaining control of small countries like Vietnam, they would soon threaten Los Angeles and San Francisco. "The Communists win in Vietnam it'll just be Laos, Thailand, the Philippines, and then we'll have to fight in California,"[2] was a typical statement made by at least one patriotic young man.

Involved in a cold war with the Soviet Union and China, and believing it was his duty to stop the spread of Communism, President John F. Kennedy decided that it would take more then just a handful of advisors to preserve Vietnam's freedom from Communism. From 1961 to 1963, thousands of American troops—Green Beret teams, counterinsurgency experts, aspiring young officers, and a small number of infantrymen—were sent to train the South Vietnamese to fight. Most Americans were unaware that U.S. "advisors" planned and led attacks against Communist forces as well.

Marines, followed by a TV crew, charge a sniper. Television brought the fighting in Vietnam into the homes of millions of Americans.

Bombing raids came next. "I don't know what the U.S. is doing," wrote one disgruntled pilot to his wife. "They tell you people we're just in a training situation. . . . But we're at war. We are doing the flying and fighting. We are losing. Morale is very bad."[3]

To make better progress, two battalions of American marines splashed ashore near Da Nang in 1965. These were younger, less experienced men, happy to serve their

A Frustrating War

Even before U.S. combat troops were sent to Vietnam, American advisors fought in an unofficial, undeclared war against the Communists. Air Force Captain Edwin Gerald "Jerry" Shank Jr. flew bombing missions during those early years and experienced much of the frustration with the war that later troops felt. A letter he sent to his wife in early 1964 is reprinted in *Reporting Vietnam,* an anthology of articles published during the war. Shank was killed in combat in March 1964.

> I have never been so lonely, unhappy, disappointed, frustrated in my whole life. . . . I am over here to do the best job possible for my country—yet my country will do nothing for me or any of my buddies or even for itself. I love America. My country is the best, but it is soft and has no guts about it at all.
>
> I'm sure nothing will be done over here until after the [U.S. presidential] elections. Why? Because votes are more important than my life or any of my buddies' lives. What gets me the most is that they won't tell you people what we do over here. I'll bet you that anyone you talk to does not know that American pilots fight this war. We—me and my buddies—do everything. The Vietnamese "students" we have on board are airmen basics. The only reason they are on board is in case we crash there is one American "adviser" and one Vietnamese "student." They're stupid, ignorant sacrificial lambs, and I have no use for them.

An American pilot in a bomber over Vietnam. The American military had been carrying out bombing missions against the Communists years before combat troops arrived.

country and fight for democracy, but woefully ignorant of Vietnam's long and colorful history. They also could not know what the war would become—a long, bitter contest that cost the United States over $150 billion, involved 3 million American men and women, and took approximately fifty-eight thousand American lives.

"By the Numbers"

Despite a willingness to serve, most of these troops—and others who followed over the years—found the Vietnam conflict to be enormously frustrating. War was never officially declared by the United States, and the government never seemed to get its heart into winning. Leadership was poor, hampered by well-meaning but overcautious politicians. Objectives were undefined. Battle plans were limited. There were no fronts and few definitive victories.

Soldiers discovered that their purpose was not to capture and hold territory, protect civilian populations, or win the support of the people, but simply to kill as many of the enemy as possible. It was war "by the numbers," and the body count—the number of enemy killed—was the only reckoning of progress. Vietnam vet (veteran) Philip Camputo writes, "Our mission was . . . simply to kill: to kill Communists and to kill as many of them as possible. Stack 'em like cordwood. Victory was a high body-count, defeat a low kill-ratio, war a matter of arithmetic."[4]

Eventually everyone—government officials, military leaders, ordinary Americans,

and soldiers in the field—came to the conclusion that the war was unwinnable unless the United States was willing to take decisive action such as it had done in Japan at the end of World War II. All agreed that such action might lead to nuclear war, an unthinkable scenario. America decided it had to get out of Vietnam.

Led by President Richard M. Nixon, the nation hoped for withdrawal with honor—that is, without total defeat—a task that proved difficult and time-consuming. Diplomatic negotiations eventually yielded an uneasy peace in late January, 1973, and Nixon seized the opportunity to bring ground troops home. The last American combat soldier left in March of that year.

Fighting between the South Vietnamese army and Vietnamese Communist forces continued until 1975, but for the United States, the war was over. Americans had had enough of Vietnam. They did not want to read about it in their newspapers or see it on television anymore. "I personally can't see that we accomplished anything," says one Vietnam veteran in retrospect. Another notes, "A lot of people want to make sure that we don't engage in that type of situation again."[5]

Postwar Suffering

As America tried to relegate Vietnam to history, soldiers who fought there discovered that they could not easily forget the war. They had shed their blood, witnessed atrocities, lost friends, and lived with horror and brutality for months on end. Coming

Different World

The American men and women who served in the Vietnam War were as diverse as the nation that produced them. Most were young, patriotic, and totally unprepared for the world awaiting them across the Pacific, as veteran, author, and editor Bernard Edelman describes in *Dear America: Letters Home from Vietnam.*

> We came 10,000 miles, almost 3 million of us, to fight America's longest war. When we arrived—on the beach at Da Nang, at the bustling air terminal of Tan So Nhut, in the baking heat of Cam Ranh Bay—we were trim and eager, jaunty and scared. But mostly, we were young. White and Black, Hispanic and Native American, Guamian and Hawaiian, the majority of us were not yet out of our teens. . . .

During the rapid build-up of American forces in the wake of the 1964 Gulf of Tonkin resolution, entire units were shipped to Vietnam. Some were greeted by "friendlies" bearing wreathes of flowers, others by sniper fire. Later, though, most of us . . . were sent as replacements, to be assigned individually to units after arriving in the country. Once assigned, we plunged into the routines of our jobs, slogging through jungles and rice paddies; skying over land cratered and defoliated, lush and green, in helicopters and jet fighters and bombers; saving lives of the traumatically injured in evacuation hospitals; cooking and clerking, writing reports and clearing land from the [Mekong] Delta to the DMZ [Demilitarized Zone].

We soon found ourselves caught up, as Lieutenant Robert Salerni put it, "in a war of contrasts in a land of contrasts," where few things were as they seemed. The Vietnamese were at once friendly and deceptive, alluring and treacherous. The weather was broiling and chilling, dusty and muddy. Even the language was different: titi and boo-boo, claymores and bangalores, dustoffs and flechettes, Hueys and Willie Pete.

Some of the first troops to arrive in Vietnam, a foreign land for which many were unprepared.

home, they fought their own private demons of anger, depression, and disillusionment, while dealing with the knowledge that they were outcasts, blamed and despised for their participation in the unpopular conflict. "I felt like the man from Mars visiting the Earth," says one soldier who naively walked down the streets of one California city wearing his uniform. "Everybody was looking at me. All kinds of comments. People spit at me. I was more scared walking down that street than I had been in Vietnam. . . . These people looked like they wanted to kill me more than the Viet Cong did."[6]

The men and women who fought in Vietnam came from various backgrounds and held a variety of attitudes and prejudices. They shared a common bond of suffering during the war, but each person's experience was unique. Each responded to the horror and inhumanity in his or her own way. Veteran and author Al Santoli writes, "It must always be remembered that the Vietnam War was a human ordeal and not an abstract heroic adventure. . . . Until the broader public fully comprehends the nameless soldier, . . . the nation's resolution of the experience called Vietnam will be less than adequate."[7]

Chapter 1

Call to Fight

The young men and women who served in Vietnam were drawn from every state in the Union—Alaska to Florida, Hawaii to Maine. Some were small-town kids from rural communities like Clayton, Kansas, and Nickerson, Nebraska. Others had grown up street- wise in urban centers like Chicago and New York City. A number came from American territories— Puerto Rico, Guam, the U.S. Virgin Islands, American Samoa, and the Panama Canal Zone.

Young and Inexperienced

Most who served were teens just out of high school. They wore blue jeans, played football, listened to rock and roll, and sometimes got into trouble on Saturday nights. Full of energy and enthusiasm, they were not quite ready to settle down to the humdrum world of work that their fathers and mothers represented. The military, with its promises of travel and adventure, was a welcome option for some, especially when

friends were signing up, too. "We all ended up going into the service about the same time—the whole crowd," remembers one who volunteered. "Four got drafted by the army. Fourteen or fifteen of us went into the Marine Corps. Out of them fourteen or fifteen . . . six of us went to Nam."[8]

Over seventy-five hundred women served in the military in the Vietnam War. A similar number of female civilians also worked in the Red Cross, United Service Organizations (USO), and other service-related positions. Some were career women over forty, but most were young, patriotic volunteers who were new to the military. They trained as air-traffic controllers, language specialists, and in security and administrative positions. Many were nurses. Cheryl Nicol, who served in Vietnam from 1967 to 1968, says, "I went into the Army in March of '66. I was living in Delaware, working in an absolutely nowhere job, and I watched one too many Huntley-Brinkley news reports. They showed some field hospitals and things like that, and I decided that I wanted and should go to Vietnam."[9]

What Americans Did Not Know

Although patriotic and eager, young Americans were woefully ignorant of the tiny nation which lay thousands of miles across the Pacific Ocean. Most did not know that the country had a long history of foreign rule, having been conquered and controlled by the Chinese, by the French (who called the region Indochina), and by the Japanese. Most did not know that the Vietnamese longed above all else for independence and to be rid of outside invaders—including well-meaning Americans—who did not un-

derstand or appreciate customs and life-styles that were so very different from those common in the West.

In fact, many Vietnamese were willing to do almost anything, make any sacrifice, to rid themselves of the outsiders who occupied and controlled their land. "If they force us into war, we will fight," said Ho Chi Minh, leader in the struggle for independence in the north. "The struggle will be atrocious, but the Vietnamese people will suffer anything rather than renounce their freedom."[10]

Few Americans were aware that Ho Chi Minh's army had already fought and won the Indochina War that began when Ho, a North Vietnamese nationalist and Com-

To Help the World

Young women often joined the military specifically so they could go to Vietnam. Christine McGinley Schneider, who worked in an evacuation hospital in Da Nang from June 1970 to 1971, relates her decision-making process in Keith Walker's *A Piece of My Heart,* the stories of twenty-six women who served in the war.

I was twenty-one years old when I went over there. I had gone through a three-year nursing program at the County Hospital in Los Angeles, and at that time there had been recruiters coming to the hospitals talking about the war, talking about the need for nurses; so that was in the back of my mind. My mom had been a Navy nurse during World War II, and I think that had a lot of impact on my decision. Then when you come out of school, you kind of feel like you want to do something to save or help the world. When I got out of school it

wasn't "Should I or shouldn't I?"—I really wanted to go, but I didn't feel like I had enough experience as a nurse. So I told myself, "I'll stay here at the County Hospital and work for a year and if I still feel this way, I'll go." I chose to work on the jail ward because they had a lot of injuries and gunshot wounds. I worked there for a year, and feeling that I still wanted to go, there wasn't any question—I was going to go.

I looked into the Red Cross and civilian organizations and none of them was sending nurses at that time. The Navy said that I would have to stay stateside eighteen months before they would consider my request for over there. The Air Force said the same thing, but when I went to the Army they promised me that I could go over immediately, and they gave it to me in writing. So I joined the Army.

An army nurse opens a bottle of rubbing alcohol to treat a young Vietnamese villager.

munist, declared his nation's independence from France in 1946. The French, who had colonized Vietnam in the 1880s, battled to remain in control and defeat the Communists, but were no match for Ho's guerrilla army. The powerful French army was finally defeated at Dien Bien Phu in northwestern Vietnam in May 1954.

First American Casualties

To help fight Communism, America had sent money and advisors to aid France in its Indochina War in the late 1940s and early 1950s. After France's defeat in 1954, peace accords divided Vietnam into North and South Vietnam, and Ho Chi Minh's Communist government secured control of the North. A free government led by Prime Minister Ngo Dinh Diem was established in South Vietnam (formally known as the Republic of Vietnam); it was supported by the United States and other Western powers as well as many South Vietnamese who hated the philosophy and tac-

and advise the South Vietnamese army (Army of the Republic of Vietnam or ARVN) in its efforts to stave off a Communist takeover.

These efforts evolved into American combat missions and led to the first hostilities against Americans in South Vietnam. In 1959, advisors Major Dale Buis and Master Sergeant Chester Ovnant were killed when members of the Viet Cong (the military's derogatory term for South Vietnamese Communist fighters) attacked a U.S. military base near Bien Hoa. Buis and Ovnant were the first U.S. soldiers to die in the Vietnam War.

The Domino Theory

By the mid-1960s, the Vietnam War was in full swing. The United States was sending large numbers of combat troops to South Vietnam to defeat the Communists, despite the fact that the North Vietnamese army was seasoned in warfare and the Viet Cong had many advantages when it came to fighting in their own country. "My God, we're whipping a dead horse,"[11] thought Taras Popel, a draftee from Chicago who looked up Vietnam in the *Encyclopaedia Britannica* and learned that America was trying to achieve what the French had failed to do in the Indochina War.

America believed it had a sound reason to exert its military might in South Vietnam, however. The Soviet Union, Communist-led since about 1922, was an expanding world power, and China had fallen under Communist rule after World

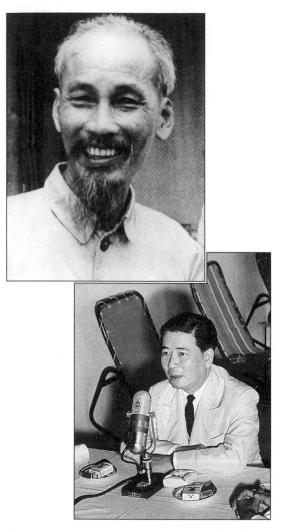

North Vietnamese Communist leader Ho Chi Minh (top) and Ngo Dinh Diem (bottom), president of South Vietnam.

tics of the Communists. Because Ho wanted to unite all of Vietnam under a Communist regime, President Dwight Eisenhower continued to send money and a limited number of troops to help train

War II. The Cold War—political tension and military rivalry—that ensued between these Communist countries and free nations in the 1950s and 1960s threatened the fate of the entire world. Nuclear war appeared a very real possibility.

So did further Communist expansion into other countries. Ho Chi Minh was intent on bringing South Vietnam under Communist control, and America's leaders believed if South Vietnam fell to the Communists, neighboring regions—Laos, Cambodia, all of Southeast Asia, and finally the United States—would come under attack and topple as well. This belief was termed the "domino theory" and was widely held by many ordinary Americans such as Lance Corporal Jack S. Swender. He wrote to his family from Vietnam in 1965:

The way I see the situation, I would rather fight to stop Communism in South Vietnam than in Kincaid, Humbolt, Blue Mound or Kansas City, and that is just about what it would end up being. The price of victory is high . . . but I think it is far better to fight and die for freedom than to live under oppression and fear.[12]

A Tradition of Service

America's youth had little interest in the history of Vietnam, but they were aware that it was admirable to be patriotic, to serve one's country proudly, and to be ready to sacrifice to protect the world against aggression and tyranny. As chil-

dren, they had played war games with friends, watched Walt Disney's Davy Crockett fight and die at the Alamo, enjoyed John Wayne and Audie Murphy movies, and dreamed of being heroes. "One of my fantasies as a kid was to be in command of a battleship in a major sea battle, and having somewhere in my sea chest Great-uncle Arthur's Naval dress sword from the eighteenth century,"[13] remembers one Vietnam veteran.

Being a war hero was more than just fantasy, however. In many households, a father had fought in World War II, or an uncle in the Korean conflict. Fighting for one's country was usually a proud part of family history, and just as parents had served in prior wars, sons were expected to do the same. Vietnam vet Todd Dasher explains, "My father and his peer group talked about World War Two and Korea and how 'this one was there' and 'that one was there' and . . . it was the right thing to do. There wasn't any question as to whether you were going to do it or not. It's part of life. There'd be something wrong with you if you didn't go in."[14]

Signing Up

Any healthy, able-bodied man between the ages of eighteen and a half and thirty-five was eligible to join the U.S. Army, although the average age of a soldier in Vietnam was nineteen. Seventeen year olds, too young to join on their own, had to get the consent of a parent or guardian in order to enlist (and could not serve in combat until they were eighteen), but most parents willingly assented.

There were plenty of reasons for enlisting in the military in the 1960s other than family tradition. Some viewed the military as an opportunity to learn a trade, to get away from home, or to prove oneself. "I thought about going to college and I really wanted to be a pediatrician. I really had those thoughts. But I just had to prove to me and most everyone else I guess, what I was made of,"[15] explains one veteran. Those who were very poor saw the army as

a chance for self-advancement, with the added benefits of steady pay, a warm bunk, and plenty to eat.

Some young men signed up because they were bored, some because they were unhappy at home. Some enlisted because they had been classified 1-A in the draft, were first in line to be called, and did not like the feeling of having their lives on

A 1971 photo of young Americans being sworn in during their enlistment process. Many enlistees volunteered for service instead of waiting to be drafted.

hold. "You knew damn well you were going to get drafted," says one. "And you're young and naive so you figure that by enlisting you might get an easy out. The next thing you know you end up in Vietnam."[16]

A few joined rather than go to jail. One vet remembers:

> In boot camp I didn't meet very many patriots. They were guys that a judge had told, "Either you go in the Army, or it's two years for grand theft auto." Or they were schmucks [fools] like me who managed to lose their deferments. Or they were people who really had decided that the Army would be good for them in the long run.[17]

The Draft

Enlistment in the army required a three-year commitment of service, the air force and navy four years. The Marine Corps allowed a minimum enlistment of two years—but it was the service branch that did the bulk of the fighting in Vietnam, so enlistees knew they would probably see combat. Draftees into the army (as compared to enlistees) were asked to serve only a two-year stint, so a great number of those who served in Vietnam waited to be called up. "I hoped I'd be able to last out two years and get back," says one man. "I wanted to get the damned thing over with and get back to my life."[18] After 1968, when peace talks and troop withdrawals were regularly in the news, even more eligible young men waited to be drafted in the

Letter from the President

Many young men had no notion of what they were getting into when they responded to their draft call. Jonathan Polansky, who served as a rifleman in the 101st Airborne Division in Vietnam from 1968 to 1969, recounts his almost passive acceptance of his induction experience in Al Santoli's oral history of the war, *Everything We Had.*

> In May of '68 I was working a small job in a mail-order house. I went home one afternoon, walked up to my bedroom and saw a letter on the bed. My father yelled, "Jon, you got a letter. I think it's from the President." I remember picking up that letter, looking at it and just sitting down, not believing it. I had to report in seven days to Whitehall Street (in New York City).
>
> We had the physical examinations and were told to report back five days later. Thousands of us. We came with nothing. They marched us down into the subway, took us to Penn Station, threw us all on trains down to South Carolina. When we got there they gave us those little [post]cards that are preprinted, saying "I am fine and I am in Fort Jackson, Carolina." They told us, "Sign your name and address on it."
>
> Well, my father, of course, was pleased as punch. He wanted to see me go. I was sort of kicking around. He thought that would shape me up, make a man out of me. . . . There was really no conception of the war. My father and I never really spoke about it. I grew up with a total lack of current events. I was never interested in the newspaper, and if I did turn on the tube it was to watch *Superman.* The question of not going into the Army never entered my mind because not many alternatives were available.

hope that the war might be over by the time they were finally called up and trained.

The draft, formally known as the Selective Service System, was designed to supply the military with sufficient personnel to ensure the security of the United States. Just prior to turning eighteen, a young man was required to register with the Selective Service. Shortly thereafter he would receive his draft status: Class 1-A (available for service); Class 2-S (student deferment/postponement of service); Class 4-F (physically or mentally unfit to serve); Class 2-A (performing a job essential to the national interest); Class 1-O (conscientious objector). Because the national voting age was twenty-one prior to 1971, most American troops who went to Vietnam were not old enough to vote for the presidents who sent them into war.

The national head of the Selective Service was appointed by the president, but local draft boards had the real authority to decide who would be inducted and who would be exempt. These local boards were made up of volunteers, usually conservative, middle-class, middle-aged, white men. Until 1967, women were prohibited from serving on draft boards because General Lewis B. Hershey, director of the Selective Service System from 1941 to 1970, "feared they would be embarrassed when a physical question emerged." [19]

Local draft committees met only once a month and had little time to give careful attention to the hundreds of names that came over their desks. Thus, only those young men with clear reasons for deferment, with economic clout, or with social connections had a chance to avoid the draft. No national standard existed, so wide variations in rulings from one board to the next were also common. For instance, the grade point average required to maintain a student deferment varied from board to board—young men making Cs and Ds in college might be granted deferments at one board, while other young men with the same grades would lose their deferments at another.

Avoiding the Draft

While poor and working-class males saw the military as a likely route to adventure or success, middle- and upper-class young men—those who objected to the war or those with college and a bright career ahead of them—tended to see military service as something to be avoided. Some flouted the law and went to prison or fled to Canada or other foreign countries rather than respond to a draft call.

Others chose legitimate ways to avoid service. A student deferment was highly popular. If a college student carried a full course-load and kept his grades up, he could stay out of the military for at least four years, more if he decided to pursue higher degrees. Filing as a conscientious objector—declaring oneself morally opposed to war—was another option that grew in popularity as the war became increasingly unpopular.

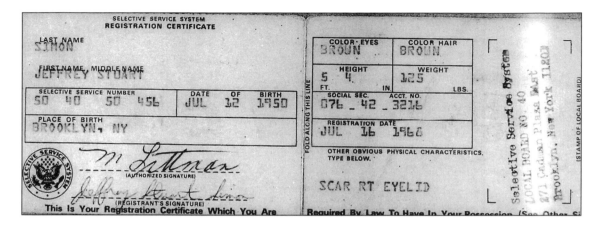

A physical exemption was a third avenue of escape. A doctor's note describing even a minor disability such as a skin rash or flat feet was often accepted by a draft board as grounds for a 4-F classification. In some cases, young men were pronounced exempt simply because they *possessed* a note, regardless of what the note said. One college graduate says, "Most of my college friends found easy paths away from the problem, all to their credit. Deferments for this or that. Letters from doctors or chaplains. It was hard to find people who had to think much about the problem."[20]

In fact, middle- and upper-class men were knowledgeable and adept at keeping out of the military; one survey showed that only about one-fifth of enlisted men in all branches of the service came from white-collar backgrounds in 1964. The preponderance of those who served in Vietnam were from the working class—the sons of farmers, factory workers, truck drivers, barbers, secretaries, police officers, and the like who lacked the means to get defer-

ments for their sons. Blacks were overrepresented in proportion to the entire U.S. population because of their economic status and because they viewed the military as a good chance for social improvement. One father, a firefighter who lost his son in Vietnam, said it well:

It's people like us who give up our sons for the country. The business people, . . . the college types, . . . their sons, they don't end up in the swamps over there, in Vietnam. No sir. They're deferred, because they're in school. Or they get sent to safe places. . . . Let's face it: if you have a lot of money, or if you have the right connections, you don't end up on a firing line in the jungle over there, not unless you *want* to.[21]

The Lottery

As the war escalated during the 1960s, draft quotas rose as high as forty thousand per month. At the same time, the war grew less popular and attitudes about serving in Vietnam changed from eagerness to resignation, then reluctance and avoidance. Young people—particularly college students who objected to the war on moral grounds—started to notice and complain about the injustices inherent in the existing draft system. Journalist Stewart Alsop wrote in 1970, "Last year . . . out of 283,000 men drafted only 28,500 were college men—just over 10 per cent. . . . The figures speak for themselves—if you can manage to go to college, your chances of not being drafted are quadrupled."[22]

In an attempt to ease some of the inequities, the government instituted a draft lottery which established a random selection sequence for induction into the military. The first lottery was held on December 1, 1969. From then on, order of induction into the military depended on a chance drawing of birth dates. Those men between the ages of 18 and 26, whose birth date was paired with the number one were the first to be inducted, those paired with the number two would be the second to be chosen for service, and so on down the line to the highest number needed to fill the draft quota. The first third of all men cho-sen had a good chance of being called; those in the middle were uncertain; those in the final third could possibly escape induction.

Some deferments were phased out, although student, occupational, and hard-ship deferments were still a possibility for many men. The lottery drawing took place every year, and draft liability lasted for one year only. Thus, if a young man was not called in one year, he was for all intents and purposes free of the threat of the draft.

Basic Training

If a young man entered the military with illusions that war was going to be a wonderful adventure, basic training dispelled that notion instantly. Upon arrival at a military base, recruits discovered that they had entered a different world where they had few rights and no privileges, where drill in-

Selective Service director General Lewis B. Hershey (behind microphone) at the first draft lottery.

structors could be tyrants, and where a man needed to be tough and obedient in order to get along.

The Marine Corps version of "basic" was the toughest and most dehumanizing of all branches of the service. From the first moment recruits arrived on base, every aspect of their lives was supervised and regulated. They were told how to eat, dress, walk, talk, salute, and a hundred other details. Bathroom privileges were limited. Conversation with each other was forbidden. Instant obedience was required. "They tore you down. They tore everything civilian out of your entire existence . . . and then they re-built you and made you over,"[23] says one Marine veteran.

The daily routine was a series of torturous drills and training exercises; the slightest sign of weakness or infraction of the rules netted severe punishment for everyone. For instance, a speck of dust on one man's shoes during inspection could send the entire platoon on a mile-long run. Throughout it all, the men were subjected to severe degradation, humiliation, and verbal abuse. "Bums," "morons," "maggots," and "scumbags" were the mildest of epithets used. Racial slurs were common. Anything that made a person different, such as being overweight or having a college education, could become a weapon in the drill sergeant's hands. Another veteran recalls,

There was a kid that had been accused of being homosexual. So consequently he was followed around by a sergeant

What Have I Gotten Into?

Basic training in the Marine Corps could be a brutal and dehumanizing experience. Young recruits, fresh from high school and a comfortable family life, were totally unprepared for the treatment they received, as one anonymous soldier explains in Mark Baker's *Nam*, an account of the war told by the men and women who fought there.

> The bus pulls into the receiving area. There's a guy with a Smokey Bear hat out there really looking lean and mean. He gets on the bus and starts, . . . "All right, you'll grab your bag. You'll get off the bus. You'll fall into the yellow footprints painted on the pavement. . . . "

> It was really funny, a take-off from *Gomer Pyle.* The guy within arm's reach of the Marine was laughing just like everybody else. Smokey Bear whipped around and smacked him right in the face, knocked him halfway through the window. His head bounced off the luggage rack and he reeled back out in the aisle.

> Smiles froze on faces. My heart stopped. We realized, "Hey this guy isn't fooling around. He's going to come through this bus and kick all our asses." People start flying out of the door. . . . We all stumble into the right footprints on the ground. . . . Smokey sees a guy's eyes flick and he's there to punch him in the chest, five feet to the wall and back again. My knees were shaking. "What . . . have I gotten myself into?"

> Then they march us into some barracks. Bare mattresses and springs. It's like a concentration camp. They turn the light on and leave us there. My stomach is in a knot. I'm lying there thinking, "What happened to my world?" . . . Kids were crying, rolling in their bunks. I'm so depressed, I can't believe this is happening to me.

and called faggot and queer and everything you can call somebody. And he was kicked, and made to crawl on his hands and knees and . . . was ridiculed in front of *everyone*. I saw that kid sitting in his bunk one afternoon and he was just rocking back and forth, banging his head against his pillow.[24]

Basic training in the army varied depending on the base and the drill sergeant. Most instructors were rigorous enough to push men to their limits. Draftees took part in drills, marksmanship training, and physical competitions that pitted man against man. The army also used ideological means—training films and lectures—to build up men's willingness to fight. Recruits were required to sit through hours of films such as *The Red Menace* and *The Anatomy of Aggression*, in which the danger of Communist expansion and invasion was made apparent in all-too-obvious detail. Army chaplains gave talks to emphasize that soldiers were honor-bound to obey orders. "The freest soldier," one chaplain read from an army manual, "is the soldier who willingly submits to authority. When you obey a lawful command you need not fear, nor worry. You can devote all your energies to getting the job done."[25]

While some army base camps were as demanding as those of the marines, a few were extremely lenient. Recruits got away with defying their instructors, skipping drills, smoking marijuana, and sleeping when they should have been working.

Reaction to Training

On all but the most lax bases, the first weeks of basic training usually focused on stripping men of their civilian identities and promoting single-minded obedience to whatever branch of the military they had joined. Recruits were worn down, broken, and exhausted. One military doctor found that stress levels, anger, and anxiety were higher in boot camp than in the front lines of Vietnam. Many young men felt lost and bewildered in such an environment. "For a long time, I was lost in the shuffle," one veteran says. "It was a shock. I never really got my bearings."[26] In some cases, the harsh treatment backfired, and men deserted, had nervous breakdowns, or tried to commit suicide.

For most young men, however, the harshness and the discipline had its desired result—they worked as hard as humanly possible to avoid humiliation and punishment, and with work came change. They learned to march with precision, to shoot straight, to think and act as an organized team. As they improved, drill sergeants barked fewer insults and encouraged pride and group spirit. One marine veteran says, "When they weren't picking on you all the time and you got over that initial fear, it was nice seeing the improvement. Man, you're marching *nice*, you're looking *good*, you're working as a *team*, you really feel that unity, that camaraderie."[27]

At some point, training began to focus on developing a deeply rooted hatred of the enemy. The rage that most recruits ini-

Marine Corps drill sergeants were extremely hard on recruits, using strict control, humiliating insults, and arduous punishments to mold the trainees.

tially channeled toward the drill sergeant was turned toward the Vietnamese Communists, who were commonly called "Charlie," "Charlie Cong," "gooks," "dinks," and "zipperheads." No one bothered to explain to trainees what the enemy was fighting for, and why they were fighting so hard. One ex-GI (General Infantry) observes, "The only thing they told us about the Viet Cong was they were gooks. They were to be killed. Nobody sits around and gives you their historical and cultural background. They're the enemy. Kill, kill, kill. That's what we got in practice. Kill, kill, kill." [28]

Following basic training, recruits were assigned to a specialized area of service such as artillery, infantry, transportation, mechanics, clerical work, cooking, or communication. While they learned the skills of a particular field, they waited to see where they would be stationed for their tour of duty. The United States had bases in Germany, England, Korea, and a dozen other spots around the world, and some young men were lucky enough to draw such prized assignments. The chances of such good fortune were relatively slim during the mid-1960s, however. One veteran remembers,

To discourage us from going AWOL [absent without leave] and deserting, all the new draftees were told that only 17 percent of us were going to Vietnam. And of that small percentage, only 11 percent would actually be combat troops. That eased my mind a great deal. Hey, there's still a chance I won't have to go and get my guts blown out. Terrific. At the end of our training, with only three exceptions—one fool who had gone Airborne, one guy who kept fainting and another kid who had a perforated eardrum—every single one of us went to Vietnam—200 guys.[29]

"Too Naive to Be Afraid"

By the time they finished training, recruits were tough, self-confident, and competent in their assigned military specialties such as firing artillery, fixing helicopters, or dressing wounds. Those that received orders to go to Vietnam had been taught certain practicalities such as the danger of poisonous snakes and punji stakes, and what to do for malaria and dysentery.

Most men, however, were still largely ignorant of the troubled little country they were going to defend. Some could not yet point out Vietnam on a map. The complexities of fighting a war against a zealous, unseen enemy were beyond their comprehension, although they would quickly gain a grasp of those difficulties. "Most of us didn't understand what was really happening in Vietnam," one former paratrooper explains. "We believed that the war had reached its final stages and that we might arrive after the last big battles were won. . . . We were too naive to be afraid."[30]

Chapter 2

"Welcome to the War, Boys"

During the early years of the war, combat soldiers arrived in South Vietnam on troop transport ships. They landed on the beaches near Da Nang and Cam Ranh Bay prepared for battle, only to find that the beaches were peaceful, and the battle was raging someplace else. Some of the first were relieved—or chagrined—to be welcomed by crews of newsmen and top U.S. military officials rather than enemy fire. "[They] were met, not by machine guns and shells, but by the mayor of Danang and a crowd of schoolgirls. The mayor made a brief welcoming speech and the girls placed flowered wreaths around the marines' necks,"[31] writes one observer.

Later troops came in cargo planes and commercial jets, the latter used in part to disguise the scale of U.S. military buildup from the American people and the world. Soldiers aboard commercial liners used jokes, laughter, and teasing to cover their nervousness and the feeling of absurdity produced by going to war in such comfort. One veteran explains:

> "Going down South," they call it in Okinawa. Braniff Airlines comes down all painted in their designer colors, puce [dark purple red] and canary yellow. There were stewardesses on the plane and air conditioning. You would think we were going to Phoenix or something. But you know that you're going to Vietnam with a plane full of marines.[32]

The reality of war hit as the plane began to make its landing. Artillery fire from below was a real danger in many locales, so pilots made fast, steep descents that brought soldiers' stomachs into their throats and all their worries to the fore. Most had not been issued weapons, and they wondered how they would defend themselves if they were immediately under attack. They had received no instructions on where to go or what to do when they got

The first troops were welcomed and greeted with flowers (above). Later, commercial planes (right) transported troops in order to hide the mounting military presence.

off the plane. Some wondered if they would be killed before they even got to the battlefield.

"A Very Weird Scene"

No planeload of soldiers was ever shot down on arrival, and landings at airports near military bases were usually peaceful. New arrivals could not banish their nervousness, however, as they saw the barbed wire and heard the thump-thump-thump of helicopters overhead. "It was just a very weird scene," says one Texas man who arrived in 1969. "I was safe, but I had no idea how safe. I had no idea what was going on or how I would fit in."[33]

Deplaning was like opening a door into a world that was unfamiliar and unpredictable. Many men noticed the intense green of the foliage, the blue of the ocean,

and the white sandy beaches. Others were struck by the heat, the oppressive humidity, and the revolting smells—dust, defoliating herbicides, rotting garbage, unwashed bodies, and animal dung—that were overpowering to sensitive American noses. One veteran observes, "When we finally touched down at Bien Hoa at midnight and they opened the door of the cabin, it was a summer like no summer I had ever known. The air rushed in like poison, hot and choking. I caught a whiff of the jungles, something dead there. I was not prepared for the heat and the smell."[34]

One of the strongest and most repulsive odors was that of human feces. Not only did many Vietnamese live without toilet facilities, but the U.S. military disposed of its tons of human waste by burning it. "What do you do if you've got 500,000 men and no plumbing facilities?" asks one man. "The army's answer . . . was to collect it in barrels . . . and set it on fire. Whoever the poor bastard was who had done something wrong yesterday, his job today was to stand there and stir this mess to make sure that it all burned."[35] Collected in fifty gallon drums under American-made outhouses, waste was liberally doused with kerosene and set afire. The smell literally filled the air, and many soldiers felt contaminated by it throughout their entire term of service in Vietnam.

Once they had deplaned and caught their breath, the most observant of the newcomers might catch a glimpse of plastic body bags that were being loaded aboard planes, mute testimony of what happened to those who were unlucky in battle. Groups of soldiers were often gathered near the runway as well, waiting to board the plane to return home. These were men who had been through a year of war; they were battle weary, cynical, foul mouthed, and old before their time. Some were on stretchers, swathed in bandages, and attended by medics.

These battered veterans appeared extremely intimidating to the newcomers because they revealed what war did to a man. Their habit of shouting insults and warnings at the new arrivals only added to the tension. "What are you gonna do, start a fight with these guys?" one soldier recalls. "We were scared out of our wits. The biggest, bad-ass guy that we had with us was shaking in his socks."[36]

"What Am I Doing Over Here?"

On arrival, troops were transported to a nearby military base. The ride emphasized the fact that danger and death were everyday realities in Vietnam. Transport buses sported heavy-duty mesh wire over their windows to prevent grenades being thrown on board. Bomb craters, destroyed villages and buildings, and burnt-out vehicles could be seen along almost every road.

At processing centers on base, men received their assignments and often learned that they were replacing a man who had been killed or wounded. Before that truth even sunk in, danger sometimes struck. One veteran remembers,

There wasn't much to do except hang around and play a little pool, waiting for our assignment. The enlisted men had to have some kind of formation every morning. They'd have all these guys lined up for role call, I guess, and every morning Charlie dropped mortars on them. These guys got killed before they even got their orders to go wherever they were going. They just put them in a bag and sent them back home.[37]

Adding to the newcomers' trauma was the feeling that they were alone with their fears. They had left their families and

No Laughing Matter

The reality of war hit new recruits as soon as they touched down in Vietnam. For some, the experience was chilling, as medic David Ross describes in Al Santoli's *Everything We Had*.

A couple of us were just kind of hanging loose out in front of the main hospital building, which was a big corrugated-tin pre-fab. About forty new guys were lined up there to have their shot records checked before being sent to their units.

The guys were all new, their first couple of days in-country, and they were all wondering what it was going to be like. Joking, smoking cigarettes . . . it was pretty loose. I mean, nobody was saying, "Straighten up. Stand in formation," none of that. People were just kind of leaning up against the building.

All of sudden, four choppers came in and they didn't even touch down. They just dumped bags. One of the bags broke open and what came out was hardly recognizable as a human being. . . . All the guys stopped laughing. Nobody was saying anything. And some people were shaking and some people were throwing up, and one guy got down and started to pray.

I said to myself, "Welcome to the war, boys."

The sight of a body bag was just one of the disturbing realities of life in Vietnam.

friends behind. Most had not transferred as a unit from boot camp into the field; rather, an individual was usually dropped into a vacancy in a preexisting fighting unit, making him a "new guy" and adding to his sense of isolation. One veteran recalls asking himself, "What was I doing over here? . . . I've forgotten everything I ever learned. I'm supposed to know how to call in artillery, I can't remember nothing. Oh my God, this is bigger than anything I ever imagined." [38]

Freshly arrived soldiers are processed into their new unit.

The Fighting Unit

For most eighteen-year-old newcomers, becoming a part of a combat unit was the first step into a world that was frighteningly different from the United States. Dropped into field camps by truck, plane, and helicopter, some men joined their units in the middle of a pitched battle where guns blazed and the dead lay strewn about like leaves. Some newcomers threw up or wet their pants from fear, but no one had time to notice or sympathize.

Others had time to get their bearings, to toss their belongings in a "hooch" (tent or shack) and to meet other GIs who had experienced combat. Even the kindest of these were war hardened—crude, superior, and scornful of "twinks," "greenies," "cherries," or "FNGs" (F—— New Guys) for their naïveté and inexperience. Reminded at every turn of their ignorance, most new-comers were grateful for any consideration they received from these tough veterans. One man remembers an incident when he and his unit came under fire shortly after he joined them.

> It was pitch black in the bunker and nobody was saying anything for awhile. Out of the silence and the darkness somebody said, "Where's the new guy?" "I'm here," I said. That was that, but there was something about that little exchange in the dark I will never forget as long as I live. The question in the dark was authentically—I don't know what the word is—generous? Caring is too big a word somehow. Generous is enough. That's a lot. That somebody even bothered to think about me. . . . I was amazed. [39]

The stresses of war evoked a strong sense of loyalty among men in a combat unit. Men relied on each other for support and camaraderie; some of the closest and most meaningful friendships in a man's life were forged in the jungles of Nam. Men unwittingly revealed their strengths and their shortcomings to each other when they were alone in the wilderness. Fighting to stay alive bonded soldiers in a unit more tightly than any other event could do. A group that began as a collection of individuals was brought together by tragedy and hard times until members were often closer than they had ever been with families and old friends. One man recalls:

> At first you got all these funky types of personalities hooking up into one military unit. Everybody had their own little hatreds, their own little prejudices, biases. But after four, five, six months that disappeared. You just saw total unity and total harmony. . . . That was the only thing that really turned me on in Vietnam. That was the only thing in Vietnam that had any meaning.[40]

The Price of Friendship

Friendships were treasured, but conditions in Vietnam could discourage too much camaraderie. Fighting units were fluid—men were always rotating in and out due to death, injury, or because their one-year term of service had expired—so members had only a short time to form a sense of community.

Hesitation to accept newcomers sprang from a sense of self-preservation as well. Inexperienced new men on patrol with their unit were often incredibly awkward and dangerous as they struggled through jungles and rice paddies carrying a heavy gun and pounds of gear. Accidents were common when men tripped, got tangled in brush or vines, and accidentally discharged their weapon. Some shot themselves. Some shot the man on the path ahead.

If the new guy happened to be a commander of the unit, results could be even more serious, as was the case when a green lieutenant called in the wrong coordinates and brought U.S. artillery fire crashing down on his own men instead of the enemy. Authors Peter Goldman and Tony Fuller describe such an incident that decimated Charlie Company, an army infantry unit, in the late 1960s.

> Whitey White got hit, and Little Brother Pierce, and one guy was missing a piece out of the top of his head, and another . . . had a gaping hole in his leg. One of the twinks was spilling tears for a lost friend, wailing, "He's dead! My buddy's dead!" Another, a black kid, was staring at the bloody stumps of three fingers, asking over and over, "What's going on?"[41]

"Friendly fire"—accidental attacks on troops by their own side—was a very real danger both in combat and behind the lines. One Pentagon study concluded

"Follow Me"

Being a new man in a seasoned combat unit was a difficult experience, especially for those in leadership positions. In Al Santoli's *Everything We Had,* Robert Santos recounts not only the difficulties, but also the embarrassment he felt as a young and inexperienced lieutenant heading up patrols near the city of Hue in 1967–1968.

I was twenty-one. But I was young in terms of commanding men in combat. I didn't know anything. I was the kind of lieutenant that they'd say, "Oh, [s——], here comes another green lieutenant." That's what I was. . . .

Everyplace I walked something got caught. You know, guys could walk right through a bush. My helmet would fall off, my pack would get snagged. And although no one ever told me, I had a reputation as the wait-a-minute-lieutenant. "Hold up, hold up, the lieutenant's caught." Here you're trying to lead men in combat and be a tough guy. Most of the guys were bigger than me. I weighed like 130 pounds. And really, always getting snagged was embarrassing.

I remember walking through the rice paddies. . . . All of a sudden all hell opened up. You have to understand, I've never been a Boy Scout, I've never been a Cub Scout. . . . I grew up in New York City and Long Island. I never fired a weapon. . . . [But] they opened up fire and . . . you make a connection real fast that someone's being shot and someone's getting hurt. . . .

The first thing I did was yell "Follow me," and I turned to the right to run for cover. . . . As I ran forward I heard these noises. Kind of like *ping, ping*—no idea what that noise was. . . . I got up and ran around yelling, "Move this machine gun over here," and "Do this over there." I mean, all this noise is going past me. I still didn't know what the noise was. *Ping.* Just a little weird, something new. I finally got back after running around, sat down next to the RTO [radiotelephone operator] and he said . . . "Don't you know what that noise is?" I said no. He said, "That's the bullets going over your head." I never knew it. I mean, if I'd known it I probably would've just buried myself and hid. But I didn't know it. I just didn't know it.

Soldiers tramp through the thick tangle of jungle growth, a challenging environment for the new arrivals.

that up to 20 percent of all U.S. casualties in Vietnam were caused by friendly fire.

Lessons and Initiation Rites

Despite the risks, many good-hearted veterans kept an eye on the new guy in the unit, and in a rough-and-ready way, taught him the vital lessons of survival—how and where to walk on patrol, when to be aggressive and when to lie low, when to ignore an order, who to trust, and who to avoid. Instruction was often a blunt word or two of advice, like that given by one young squad leader to his unseasoned men: "Keep low and keep straight and don't do nothing crazy. . . . If the [fighting starts], keep your ass down and keep firing. You don't even have to look, just keep . . . firing. Somebody'll help you out. One of these days, you'll help one of us out." [42]

At other times the lesson was a shocking initiation rite. On his first day, one newcomer was surrounded by his unit and urged to kick a dead Vietnamese soldier to pieces in order to toughen himself for the barbarity that was an integral part of the war. He later wrote:

> They were serious men, dedicated to what they were doing. At that time the dedication was to teaching me, to preparing me for when death do strike . . . not to fall apart if a friend dies. I saw it happen. I saw guys get themselves killed and almost get an

New troops learning combat tactics were instructed to stay low and keep firing.

entire platoon wiped out, because they panicked or because they gave up or because they got wounded and couldn't deal with their own blood. They had this thing about teaching a boot [new guy] exactly what he's got to deal with and how to accept the fact of where he really is. [43]

Drugs such as marijuana and heroin were another means by which seasoned GIs helped newcomers cope with the shocking realities of the war. While the vast majority of young men had never touched drugs before leaving the United States, over 50 percent of troops used marijuana before the war was over. One veteran remembers his first experience with pot: "I was sitting in

Battle Tested

New men became experienced veterans as they lived through battles and earned the respect of their comrades. In Mark Baker's compelling work, *Nam,* an unnamed veteran gives a glimpse of this toughening process, and the event that established his reputation.

> We went on Search and Destroy patrols. The helicopters would pick us up early in the morning and fly us out someplace, set us down and we'd spend a whole day walking around. Most of the time nothing happened.
>
> We did get into a few fire fights. But what was taking place was so much less terrifying than the pitched battles I had imagined in my head that the level of fear was just not that high.
>
> "Shoot, shoot," people kept saying to me.
>
> "Where are they?"
>
> "They're over there," they would say, pointing in the general direction of some trees about 150 yards away. So I would edge up over the top of a rice paddy dike and I would shoot at the tree line. All right, now I've shot. I'm done with that. . . .
>
> Eventually, I was regarded as being "okay." I'd been through some fire fights and I didn't freeze up. . . . One incident really cinched it for me. In one fire fight there was nothing for me to do. We were crouched behind a dike and weren't in any danger, unless we did something stupid like stand up and charge a machine gun nest, which I wasn't about to do. I fell asleep in the middle of the whole thing. That was considered cool. I became one of the guys—Battle Tested.

Soldiers under attack take cover. Living through the fire fights turned inexperienced men into battle-hardened veterans.

this bunker feeling very happy—completely stoned, and all of a sudden something exploded. . . . When they grabbed me and told me we were under attack my mind started to race—'Oh God no, I'm going to die. The first time in my life I get stoned and I'm going to die.'"[44]

Becoming a Veteran

There was no hard-and-fast rule for when a newcomer turned into a seasoned soldier in Vietnam. Each man's experience was different. Some men seemed to understand the job they were called to do and learned it quickly. Others never adjusted, never learned, and often endangered themselves and others due to their ineptness. For most, however, time and experience erased the naïveté. Veteran James Bombard says:

What I found was after the first fire fight they were all veterans. They lost that greenness immediately. Usually the first fire fight consisted not only of a fight but also so many days in the jungle putting the skills of a soldier to use—walking in the jungle, being scared, setting up defenses, perimeters. It was thinking about survival, and all of a sudden, BOOM, you were a soldier, you were a veteran.[45]

As they lost their greenness, newcomers came to terms with the terrible reality of Vietnam where death was everywhere, where fear was as real as bullets, and where the dark side of a man's character had every opportunity to develop. The war was brutalizing, and there was no legitimate way to escape the horror, the revulsion, and the never-ending bloodshed that their government demanded of them.

It was very much like being sentenced to a large, green prison where one had to kill or be killed. One man observes, "Humping [walking combat patrol] in the Nam was like being on a chain-gang, only the prisoners all got to hold rifles just like the guards."[46] There was only one option for most soldiers: to learn enough of the tricks of fighting and survival to get by until one's sentence expired. For better or worse, that is what most of them did.

Chapter 3

"Humping the Boonies"

Foot soldiers, nicknamed "grunts," were given a variety of assignments once they arrived in Vietnam, but all tasks dovetailed into one primary purpose—to kill as many of the enemy as possible. Body counts and kill ratios—the number of enemy dead compared to American dead—were the means by which victories were declared and progress assessed. One veteran recalls, "What I thought it was going to be and what it turned out to be were so totally different. There was no romance at all in it. Absolutely none. That was stripped bare immediately."[47]

Because pressure from military commanders was great, the figures were regularly adjusted to make a good impression. Numbers of Americans killed were minimized, numbers of enemy dead were exaggerated upward. Inevitably any dead Vietnamese, civilian or otherwise, was used to make up the quotas.

Killing the enemy was easier said than done. American soldiers attempted to track them down, flush them out, and kill them on long, laborious "search-and-destroy" missions. Such missions were often given formal names such as Operation Prairie or Operation Paul Revere to give them some meaning, but in fact, most were unconnected offensives, distinguishable from one another only by the heaviness of fighting or the number of enemy casualties. Most were arduous patrols through jungles and across mountains of South Vietnam, and GIs colorfully referred to the process of walking them as "humping the boonies."

A patrol could last up to thirty days. Men were transported by truck or carried by helicopter to a drop-off point, where arrival was always a nerve-racking moment. The landing zone might be "cold"—peaceful and deserted—or "hot," with the enemy firing as soon as the grunts set foot on the ground.

Jets and gunship helicopters did their part to ensure the GIs' safety by spraying

Hiking the Highlands

Although toughened by the rigors of boot camp, combat soldiers were unprepared for the grueling task of plodding up and down the mountains of Vietnam, searching for the enemy. They performed heroically, as one unnamed veteran describes in Mark Baker's *Nam*.

The Central Highlands is called the Highlands because there's nothing but . . . mountains everywhere. All we did was hump the mountains. My ass was kicked. We're walking up and down these hills. It must be 103 degrees and I'm dying. The heat beats you. The jungle is humid. . . .

Every day we'd hump rucksacks that weighed over a hundred pounds. There were only two people in my company who could put on a rucksack standing up. You took them off when you were facing a tree. That way when you put them back on, you were sitting on the ground, you put your arms in and you could grab the tree to get yourself off the ground. We humped these things every day, four, five, six, seven klicks [kilometers].

In the late afternoon, we'd always pull a night logger position on the highest hill within the area—for security reasons. You hump all day—which is killing you—then at three or four in the afternoon . . . you hump the biggest hill when you're already exhausted. The hills were steep. Many times the person in front of me going up the hill, his feet would be where my face was. . . .

The people that humped well looked like they were ready to have a heart attack when they were done humping. You look at a guy who has humped up a hill and he looks like he just jumped into a swimming pool and jumped back out. He was that salty and wet from the heat. You could hardly pick up your feet at the end of the day. It doesn't get any better.

Troops had to hike up and down the steep, jungle-covered mountains of Vietnam.

the area with rocket and machine-gun fire before the landing. Eventually, however, all air support returned to home base and the patrol was left alone to carry out its assignment. "When the helicopters flew off, a feeling of abandonment came over us. . . . Being Americans, we were comfortable with machines, but with the aircraft gone we were struck by the utter strangeness of this rank and rotted wilderness,"[48] one ex-GI remembers.

Left in the boonies, men spent days on end walking from one point to another from sunup to sundown. In the evening they pitched camp and set up defenses; in the morning they broke camp and set off, usually with no idea of where they were going. Their only goal was finding and eliminating the elusive enemy. "Intelligence says they're out there, so you go walking around in little geometric triangles," one man says, describing his patrol's search for the enemy. "Go to this checkpoint, go to that checkpoint, go here, go there. Day in, day out, day in, day out. You get into a mind-numbing routine."[49]

Scapegoats

Even on a mission, men often had no idea of where they were going, how far they were going, or how long they were going to be away from base. Orders, called in by radio from headquarters, could be changed at any time and often were. A unit might settle down for the night and then be told to get their equipment together and set off on a night march. "Our first mission was at night," one veteran recalls. "We were scared stiff. We headed into the jungle without any idea where we were going, or what we were doing. We kept walking for a couple of hours in the dark, praying we wouldn't lose sight of the guy in front of us."[50]

The greatest uncertainty was when the enemy would strike. Although combat units were officially on the offensive, in reality the enemy controlled the terms of battle. The Viet Cong and North Vietnamese army were made up of natives of Vietnam, who were familiar with every hill and valley,

A sense of vulnerability caused much anxiety among soldiers being dropped off at landing zones.

rock and tree. They fought as guerrillas—attacking without warning at random times and places, then disappearing into their jungle hideouts without a trace. "Humans are out there watching you," one man says. "They know where you're going before you even get there. You see them running very far away in their straw hats and black outfits."[51]

Unless grunts stumbled upon an enemy patrol and a battle ensued, most American patrols simply acted as bait, showing themselves in a region in order to lure the enemy into making an attack. "The purpose . . . was for you to walk up on Charlie and for him to hit you, and then for our hardware to wipe them out. We were used as scapegoats to find out where they were. That was all we were—bait. They couldn't find Charlie any other way,"[52] one man explains.

Electrifying Encounters

Inevitably, enemy encounters occurred, and when they did they were hair-raising, pulse-pounding events. Grenades flew, machine guns rattled, and men shouted, cursed, and dodged. As a former-GI describes:

> All hell broke loose. I dived over this log and I peeked from behind it. I hear one of these guys with me screaming at the top of his lungs. His leg is all blown to shit. The dirt is popping all around him. . . . I'm opening up with my M-16, changing magazines, trying to get that

. . . pack off my back so I can work out. I know they're up there and I'm just capping [shooting at] them.[53]

While American soldiers concentrated on shooting at anything that moved, their communication specialist radioed for backup firepower. Soon American jets and gunships roared overhead. Rockets and napalm were added to the mix.

All too often, the enemy slipped away when faced with such heavy firepower, wisely choosing to live and fight another day. Then, troops were left to catch their breath, wearily assess their losses, call for helicopters to carry out their wounded, and go on with their mission.

If the engagement was prolonged and the Americans proved victorious with a high body count, they naturally experienced a great sense of satisfaction, the conviction of a job well done. Victory offered little sense of permanent accomplishment, however. All knew that no concrete objective was ever gained, and the same battle could be fought a hundred times over the same ground. Even if a village or a region of jungle was "captured" and cleansed of hostiles, as soon as American soldiers moved on, the enemy returned, rebuilt, and reestablished himself just as if the battle had never taken place.

Test of Endurance

Since it was in the enemy's interest to avoid fiercely waged battles as much as possible, grunts spent weeks and months walking

The Horror

The reality of war—the fear, the chaos, the ugliness, and the horror of seeing men die—significantly changed many men, draining away their youth and leaving them hard and empty-eyed, as one GI describes in Mark Baker's book, *Nam*.

> The night finally ended and the dawn came. The firing stopped as it always did before dawn. Shortly after that the guys started coming back from being on guard. They had been under heavy fire for five and a half hours, nonstop. . . .
>
> Lawrence was first. His eyes were what I saw first. Eyes are what you always see first. It's hard to talk about it without being cliched. It's hard to avoid using "1,000-yard stare." What I saw in Lawrence's eyes was the horror, The Horror. . . . I don't even begin to know what those two guys went through that night.

All I know is what I saw the next morning, and all the ways that Lawrence was never the same person again.

> Lawrence hadn't been there very long. He was happy-go-lucky and naive, everybody's teddy bear. He sounded like he was from Brooklyn, but he wasn't a rough street kid. He was coming from some tough places, but somehow he was too gentle for that. . . .
>
> The guy who came back that morning was not the guy who went out twenty-four hours earlier. And he was never that person again. . . . When he did start talking again, he never spoke with the enthusiasm he had had before. His eyes were masked and dull like an old man's. They seemed to sit deeper inside his skull. If he had been wrinkled and lined, he would have been a cynical seventy-year-old man.

Numbed by the horrors he had witnessed, a war-weary soldier stares dazedly at the camera.

through jungles and rice paddies, seldom seeing a hostile Vietnamese for long periods. "War is not [just] killing," one veteran observes. "Killing is the easiest part of the whole thing. Sweating twenty-four hours a day, seeing guys drop all around you of heatstroke, not having food, not having water, sleeping only three hours a night for weeks at a time, that's what war is. Survival."[54]

Despite physical hardships, time dragged for most patrols, and boredom made soldiers irritable and prone to carelessness. There was nothing to do but think about all the good things back home—playing sports, watching television, dating, being with family—and try to ignore the weariness and fear. It was as if one were in an endurance race of unspecified length, in which the greatest test of life and limb could come in the middle, at the end, or not at all. Most often it came when least expected, as one man testifies:

> You go long periods of time just patrol after patrol after patrol for months and months and you don't run into any gooks or anything; no booby-traps, no nothing. . . . Then all of a sudden one day somebody gets killed or hits a booby-trap and gets real messed up. You learn then that you have to be alert at all times, but it's hard to do when you go long times with not running into any gooks or anything.[55]

Not surprisingly, under such conditions many men yearned for a skirmish to provide a change of pace, a reason for all the footslogging. One veteran remembers, "It was better to get into a fight than just walk about sweating."[56] Other men did not go so far, but they did agree that the endless, aimless walking was one of the hardest aspects of serving in combat in Nam.

Treacherous Terrain

Vietnam's terrain and climate were two factors that made "humping the boonies" so difficult and miserable. The land was lovely to look at, with verdant mountains, green rice fields, and tropical scenes straight from the movie *South Pacific*. One soldier wrote to his mother, "This country is so beautiful, when the sun is shining on the mountains, farmers in their rice paddies, with their water buffalo, palm trees, monkeys, birds, and even the strange insects. For a fleeting moment I wasn't in a war zone at all, just on vacation."[57]

But that same terrain was treacherous to those who did not know their way about. The Viet Cong often planted explosives around the perimeter of rice fields, so grunts learned it was safer to walk through the paddies, which were always flooded. "You had to know how to walk in the paddies. Some of them were just water waist-deep. But some of them were like a marsh with floating grass over the water. If you didn't know how to walk on it you'd sink in up to your neck,"[58] one former soldier recalls.

Jungle-covered mountains not only provided a thousand places for the enemy to hide, they were also steep, and the overgrowth and all that lived in it was entirely foreign and enormously overwhelming to outsiders, particularly boys who were used to sidewalks and city streets. Clearing a path through tangled bushes and vines often required the use of machetes or even chain saws. One man wrote in 1969,

> Anyone over here who walks more than 50 feet through elephant grass should automatically get a Purple Heart. Try to imagine grass 8 to 15 feet high so thick as to cut visibility to one yard, possessing razor-sharp edges. Then try to imagine walking through it while all around you are men . . . who desperately want to kill you. You'd be amazed at how much a man can age on one patrol.[59]

The dense jungle canopy often filtered out all sun, reducing light to a dim glow and making it difficult for men to see where to walk. No air moved, and the high humidity made breathing as labored as in a sauna. Insects inflicted dozens of bites.

Thorny vines—called "wait a minute vines" by the men—grabbed at clothes and weapons and made deep scratches on hands and faces. "It has become my opinion that the national flower of Vietnam should be an immense thorn,"[60] one man wrote home.

Monsoons, Leeches, and Sore Feet

The heat was often intense in Vietnam, reaching above one hundred degrees during the dry season—suffocating in the dank, airless jungle. Cooler weather provided a little relief, but it was accompanied by monsoons—seasonal winds and heavy

The constant walking (left) and rains of the monsoon season (above) frustrated many soldiers.

rain that lasted from April to October and dumped up to 120 inches of precipitation on unlucky soldiers. Rainfall in America averages less than 50 inches per year, so few GIs were prepared for such downpours. One veteran remembers, "Going out to an ambush one night, it rained so hard, I started to choke. I couldn't breathe. I bent over to create an airpocket under my chest. In that moment, it was filled with mosquitoes."[61]

During the monsoon season, everything—clothes, shoes, tents, even cigarettes—grew sodden and unpleasant. "Mud, I never knew how much mud I could hate," one grunt complained in a letter home. "We live in mud and rain. I'm so sick of rain that it is sometimes unbearable. At night the mosquitoes plague me while I'm lying on the ground with my poncho wrapped around me. The rain drips on me until I go to sleep from exhaustion."[62]

Leeches were a particularly nasty problem whenever grunts walked through water or had to push their way through wet foliage. The bloodsucking worms had the knack of getting up a man's trouser legs or down into his boots, where they burrowed into his flesh. Leeches caused as much emotional trauma as physical discomfort to squeamish foot soldiers. Many men grew accustomed to examining themselves during rest periods, however, and passed the time burning off the pests with lighted cigarettes.

Foot problems were more incapacitating than leeches. Soldiers walked miles a day, often in boots that did not fit and were continuously wet. "They gave me a pair of size-twelve jungle boots and I wear a size ten. My foot slid in it. . . . So the left side of my foot developed a blister, then a callous and then a planter's wart,"[63] former marine James Hebron testifies. Blisters and calluses were a fact of life for most men.

More serious was a condition known as "immersion foot," caused by having the feet submerged in water for a prolonged period. Feet swelled and grew so tender that boots had to be cut off, and skin peeled in horrifyingly large pieces. At times, men had to be helicoptered back to a base hospital after their feet cracked, bled, and became infected.

Illness and Fatigue

Foot problems were not the only threats to health that men faced. Many soldiers suffered from heatstroke and came down with malaria and other jungle illnesses. All were issued water purification tablets, designed to be dissolved in drinking water, but even those did not totally stave off problems of diarrhea and stomach cramps caused by waterborne pathogens.

Animal bites were a constant hazard, with rats being the prime annoyance. One newcomer was warned of the aggressiveness of the rodents at night, but ignored the warning. "Suddenly, this guy is yelling at the top of his lungs," a veteran recalls. "Everybody broke and jumped up with their weapons. . . . He had a hunk of meat out of his face. He had slept with his head out. He don't like to sleep with his head covered up, was his remark. . . . [A rat] just bit and took that meat out of his face."[64] Rabies was a very real threat in Vietnam, and men who were bitten often had to undergo a series of rabies shots that made their war experience that much more unpleasant.

Adding to the mix of discomfort and illness was deep, chronic fatigue. Men on patrol were always tired, yet could not give in to the weariness which increased day by day. Many felt pushed to the breaking point, as marine platoon leader David Westphall III wrote during his year in Nam.

Chronic fatigue was prevalent due to combat stress, the difficult terrain, and unrelenting heat and humidity of Vietnam.

My feet were about to crack open, my stomach knotted by hunger and diarrhea, my back feeling like a mirror made of nerves shattered in a million pieces by my flak jacket, pack, and extra mortars and machine-gun ammo, my hands a mass of hamburger from thorn cuts, and my face a mass of welts from mosquitoes. I desired greatly to throw down everything, slump into the water of the paddy, and sob.[65]

Doggie Straps, Dirt, and Bad Food

The weight of equipment a soldier carried while on patrol contributed to his pain and exhaustion. Unlike the Viet Cong, who wore light, pajama-like garments and sandals and lived off the land, GIs were equipped with a uniform, boots, flak jacket, and helmet, all of which were unbearably hot and heavy.

Soldiers sometimes risked their lives by removing flak jackets and helmets in order to cope with the heat. Those articles still had to be carried, however, as did rucksacks that could hold over one hundred pounds of supplies—including ammunition, C-rations (canned rations), bedding, water, flares, and personal items such as cigarettes, a Bible, and letter writing materials. The weight of all these things could be excruciatingly painful. Veteran James Hebron says:

Doggie straps—that was the thing we used to dream about, shoulder straps. Army wide ones to support that weight. Packs were getting tremendously heavy in this war. . . . My clutch belt must have weighed forty-five pounds with a K-bar knife on it and .45 pistol and you name it. . . . It was a real coup [achievement] to get your hands on doggie straps.[66]

Dirty clothes and dirty bodies contributed to the discomfort of the march. Men seldom had the luxury of bathing, shaving, or doing laundry while on patrol. "I've taken one shower in two months, wore the same clothes for two months, and have been sleeping on the ground in water. I guess that's why they say war is hell,"[67] wrote Robert Santos in 1968. Another veteran remembers, "I didn't brush my teeth for two months in Vietnam, the reason being that though they sent toothbrushes out in SP packs [cellophane packets containing soap, toothpaste, etc.], we had to use them to clean our rifles. There were certain things that came first."[68]

Poor food added to a GI's unhappiness. C-rations were the standard meal. They were sometimes heated over a fire, often consumed cold. "Beanies and weenies" was one entree that was tolerated by most men. Ham and lima beans were unpopular, although there were always exceptions. Former rifleman John Muir says, "We had one guy who used to like them and he used to collect all these peppers, rice and everything you could think of, and poured it all into a helmet with his ham and lima beans and mixed this ungodly concoction of stuff and he'd eat that. But he was from West Virginia and we'd take that into account."[69]

Canned fruit was a delicacy men would fight over, as in the case of a can of pears several men confiscated from a Vietnamese family. A veteran recalls, "We're fighting, literally fighting to eat pears. . . . It was like the man brought me steak and potatoes and I was back in my mother's house eating Sunday dinner."[70]

Ambushes and Booby Traps

A greater threat than all the other hazards and hardships that came with "humping the boonies" were booby traps, set by the enemy. Some of these traps were simple trip wires or hand grenades, hung at chest height and camouflaged by leaves. Some were mines, buried in the ground. One of the most infamous was the "Bouncing Betty" that did not immediately blow up when stepped on. Rather, it popped up and exploded in the air after a soldier's foot released a trigger mechanism, injuring him and those who followed behind as well.

Some traps were homemade devices made from tin cans, bottles, nails, scrap iron, and explosives gleaned from unexploded bombs and shells dropped by the Americans themselves. Many of these were ingenious creations. "One of his biggest weapons against us is a small can of peanut butter, which he makes a beautiful booby trap out of,"[71] wrote one soldier to his family. The Viet Cong also used more traditional forms of traps such as punji stakes—sharpened bamboo sticks, coated with excrement and planted at an angle in tall grass or at the bottom of pits. Such devices were designed to impale and kill the enemy or, at the very least, produce a severe wound and infection.

Even the wiliest soldiers could not spot every mine and booby trap, and on many missions, more men were injured and killed by traps and mines than were lost in battle. The constant effort to avoid the in-

visible threats produced great tension and fear among combat patrols, as former GI Tim O'Brien explains:

Should you put your foot to that flat rock or the clump of weeds to its rear? Paddy dike or water? You wish you were Tarzan, able to swing with the vines. You try to trace the footprints of the man to your front. You give it up when he curses you for following too closely; better one man dead than two. The moment-to-

Lessons out of School

Combat brought men together and forced them to cooperate in ways that they might never have done in civilian life. The war also inspired much impromptu creativity, as former combat engineer Harold "Light Bulb" Bryant describes in Wallace Terry's *Bloods,* an account of the war as told by black veterans.

This infantry unit was on a little trail, west of Pleiku, makin' a sweep towards the Ia Drang Valley. This white dude had stepped on a mine. And knew it. He felt the plunger go down. Everybody moved away from him, about 20 meters. So they called for the engineers, and somebody asked for Light Bulb.

I have a nickname from the streets of East St. Louis. Light Bulb. Came from a friend of mine when we were growing up, 'cause he said I was always full of ideas. . . .

I dug all around the mine with my bayonet and found out that it was a Bouncin' Betty. I told him I was gonna try to diffuse it. But the three-prong primer on the Bouncin' Betty had gotten in between the cleats on his jun-

gle boots, so there wasn't any way I could deal with it. So I said let's see if we could kind of change the pressure by him takin' his foot out of his boot and me keepin' the pressure by holding his boot down. That way he could get out uninjured. But when he started doin' that, I thought I was seein' the plunger rise, so I told him to stop. . . .

Then I got the idea. I knew when the plunger would depress, the Bouncin' Betty would bounce up about three feet and then explode. So I got the other members of his team together, and tied a rope around his waist. And everybody, including me, moved off about twenty yards from the mine and him. And when I counted to three, everyone would pull on the rope and snatch him about fifteen feet off the mine. And it would bounce up its three feet and then explode. And it did that. And the only damage that he received was the heel of his jungle boot was blown off. No damage to him.

This was somethin' that they never taught us in school.

moment, step-by-step decision-making preys on your mind. The effect is sometimes paralysis. You are slow to rise from rest breaks. You walk like a wooden man . . . with your eyes pinned to the dirt, spine arched, and you are shivering, shoulders hunched.[72]

Friend or Foe?

Not all operations were conducted in uninhabited regions of Vietnam. Many times, hamlets and villages lay in the zones that combat units patrolled, and then a unit's assignment was to search for and kill any members of the Viet Cong or North Vietnamese army that might be hiding among the local population.

Officially, such search-and-destroy missions were intended to protect innocent Vietnamese civilians. Military rules of conduct dictated that every U.S. soldier carry on his person a card of guidelines to which he was to adhere. These included avoiding loud and rude behavior, trying to learn some of the language, giving the Vietnamese the right-of-way, and behaving as guests in a foreign land.

In the course of time, however, patrols learned that there was no clear-cut way to tell if ordinary villagers were pro-American, communist sympathizers, or even members of the Viet Cong. All looked alike; all dressed alike. The innocent villager who worked in his rice paddy by day was sometimes an enemy sniper by night. Any ser-

North Vietnamese soldiers set up punji stakes, sharpened bamboo sticks coated with excrement and designed to impale those who stepped on them.

vant on a military base could be an informant who passed information to the Communists.

Even apparently uninvolved persons helped the enemy by providing food and shelter, or by cooperating in more subtle ways. One former marine captain recalls, "Here's a woman of twenty-two or twenty-three. She is pregnant, and she tells an interrogator that her husband works in Danang and isn't a Vietcong. But she watches your men walk down a trail and get killed or wounded by a booby trap. She knows the booby trap is there, but she doesn't warn them. Maybe she planted it herself."[73]

Not only women, but also children could be as dangerous as any male. One army nurse recalls, "Most of the GIs were suckers for little kids. They'd always pick them up. We had a little boy that was booby-trapped. He was about five years old. Somebody had put a bomb on him and sent him into a bar where there were a lot of GIs hanging out. Someone picked him up and he exploded. It killed five GIs."[74]

Even ARVN soldiers, who were America's allies, were unreliable, particularly when it came to relying on them in battle. "In a fire fight those ARVNs would drop everything and run to the rear. That's why I hate them, those Vietnamese,"[75] said one man.

This inability to tell friend from foe, coupled with the need to root out the enemy, led to widespread mistreatment of many Vietnamese. In most cases, abuse was only moderate if villagers offered no resistance. "We would go through a village before dawn, rousting everybody out of bed, and kicking down doors and dragging them out if they didn't move fast enough,"[76] veteran William Ehrhart explains. Homes were searched and set afire, animals killed, stores of rice destroyed. Village leaders were questioned and sometimes beaten. Since the Viet Cong relied on elaborate tunnel systems to evade detection, GIs made a habit of searching for dugout cellars and bunkers, and killing anyone hiding there on the assumption that they were the enemy.

Not surprisingly, such behavior alienated many civilians, as Ehrhart observes. "Their homes had been wrecked, their chickens killed, their rice confiscated—and if they weren't pro-Vietcong before we got there, they sure as hell were by the time we left."[77]

GIs considered out-and-out violence appropriate and justifiable if a village offered resistance or was known to be an enemy stronghold. In one incident in 1967, two marine companies took heavy losses and were pinned down for days by enemy fire coming out of a hamlet south of Da Nang. When the marines finally entered the settlement, they were ruthless, as one man remembers. "Our emotions were very low because we'd lost a lot of friends. . . . So when we went

Viet Cong soldiers (pictured) were not always easy to distinguish from Vietnamese civilians.

An American soldier searches a village near Bong Son for Viet Cong after an air strike during Operation Masher on January 25, 1966.

through those hutches, we gave it to them, and whoever was in a hole was going to get it. And whatever was moving was going to move no more."[78]

Short-Timers

Death of a comrade was one of the most traumatic events an American soldier experienced in the war, and nothing could totally relieve the grief that men felt when one of their own was taken. Veteran James Bombard recalls: "To see your friends

killed, hear about them being killed, . . . [a] little piece of you gets killed each time."[79]

Many men tried to shield themselves from such pain by remaining aloof, although such a stance was difficult in the emotional roller coaster of war. Others chose to be friends with everyone, but to keep a certain emotional distance. "You learn every day the mistakes you are making, and the biggest one is to get too attached to any one person,"[80] wrote veteran Donald J. Jacques, who was himself killed in action in 1968.

Another kind of loss with which everyone coped was that of a buddy leaving the unit after his one-year stint was completed. GIs willingly faced these leave-takings, however, because survival and going home was everyone's primary concern. Men usually knew precisely how many days remained in their term of service. Some kept crude calendars inside their helmets, in their Bibles, and on the linings of their flak jackets.

Members of a unit inevitably became protective of "short-timers" and "two-digit midgets"—those who had fewer than ninety-nine days of their one-year tour left to serve. If possible, squad leaders pulled strings and got them reassigned to jobs as office clerks or mechanics in the rear, far from the fighting, so their survival was ensured. The death of a short-timer was always particularly upsetting to those men in his unit who survived. Ironically, many men who had lived through incredible dangers were killed just before they were scheduled to leave Vietnam.

Life on Base

The war was dangerous and disturbing, and combat units often saw their lives as one long trek through the jungle, but there were times when existence could be relatively enjoyable. Between missions, men were allowed brief rest periods, called "stand-downs," at nearby military bases—

A soldier keeps track on his helmet the number of days left in his tour. Others drew the makeshift calendars inside their flack jackets or Bibles.

the nearest semblance to America that Vietnam offered. "Every time you came back to battalion from being on an operation, you get the day off, all the steaks, hot dogs and hamburgers you can eat, all the beer and soda you can drink. . . . Just hanging out was incredible, the feeling of life,"[81] remembers one veteran about his return from fifty-four days in the jungle.

The military did its best to supply the comforts of American society whenever possible. Large bases had electricity, and men enjoyed hot showers and freshly prepared meals. Barbecues complete with hamburgers, hot dogs, and ice cream were common. One man recalls, "The Army had it good; the Air Force, better. We had it the greatest, the Navy. We had hot and cold running water. Air conditioning. The Navy always had great food, but this base was somethin' else. . . . We ate like kings. Lobster, steak, everything. I must have gained forty pounds."[82]

Most bases had a well-stocked post exchange (PX) where men could purchase for a reasonable price everything from cigarettes to stereos to fine jewelry. Beer was cheap and plentiful. So were drugs, if a man knew whom to ask. Red Cross nurses, USO volunteers, and Vietnamese prostitutes provided at least a vestige of female companionship. Respectable Vietnamese women could also be hired as maids and laundresses—dubbed "hoochgirls" by the troops—to relieve men of irksome housekeeping duties. That gave them more time to play pool and watch television and nightly movies. American shows like *Bonanza, Star*

Trek, and *My Favorite Martian* were popular on base just as they were back in the United States.

Rest and Recuperation

Another relief from the stress of combat was the military's Rest and Recuperation (R&R) program—a benefit that gave men a real break from the war sometime after six months of service. Most GIs were given a generous allowance and sent alone or in small groups for a week at one of the major cosmopolitan centers of the east, such as Hong Kong, Honolulu, Tokyo, Singapore, or Sydney, Australia.

For men who went on R&R, the contrast between such cities and the war was shocking. After living in mud for months, they found themselves in clean clothes, walking down brightly lighted streets. Most treated themselves to lush hotel rooms, fine dinners, massage parlors, movie theaters, and anything else money could buy. One former marine remembers,

> I finally went and got a room in a hotel. The Hong Kong tailors would come up, knock on the door and say in a soft voice, "Hello, my name is Lou Chow from Kowloon, Hong Kong. We wish to give you suit now." They give you the suit just for the night so you'd come by the shop and buy one. Everybody bought suits. I got a couple or three of them for $30 apiece.[83]

Most men enjoyed R&R to the fullest, cramming every minute to the top with sex, alcohol, spending sprees, and tourist activities. The getaway experience was all too short, however, and returning to the horror of war was a blow for which few were prepared. One says, "That same night I'm back in the . . . rain and mud with leeches and people trying to kill me. That was a twist on the head. . . . It was like a hand coming out of space, picking you up and putting you on another planet for three days. I was sorry I took R&R."[84]

The Other Guys

While hundreds of thousands of GIs were allowed only brief respites from the ordeal of combat, thousands more were lucky enough to enjoy a life of relative ease and safety throughout their entire year in Nam. "There are two different wars here in Vietnam," complained some of the men of Company D, Third Battalion in 1969. "While we are out in the field living like animals, putting our lives on the line 24 hours a day, seven days a week, the guy in the rear's biggest problem is that he can receive only one television station. There is no comparison between the two."[85]

There was some truth in the complaint, but support troops—those who aided combat forces—had their own criticisms, their own problems, and their own disillusionments. No one got away without paying a price in Vietnam.

Chapter 4

Office Pogues and Green-Faced Frogmen

Not every soldier "humped the boonies" in the Vietnam War. For every man in the field, at least five served in the rear (a locale some distance from the fighting) and as backup for combat troops, performing tasks that ranged from mundane, frustrating, and frivolous to arduous, rewarding, and vital to the war's progress.

The list of jobs performed by support personnel was long. Chaplains and psychiatrists were on hand to listen, encourage, and evaluate GIs' mental health. Clerks procured supplies; engineers designed roads and landing strips; security police kept order. Doctors, nurses, and medics attended to the sick and wounded. Air crews used their bombs and rockets to bail out men pinned down by enemy fire. Special Forces units and covert operation specialists carried out secret missions and eased the burden on ordinary combat patrols in the field.

Though commonly despised by front line troops, administrative and office per-

sonnel—derogatorily called "office pogues" or "Remington's Raiders" (for the Remington typewriter)—were vital for dealing with the vast bureaucracy of military red tape and record keeping that made up the modern war. Office personnel worked in the combat soldier's best interest—ordering parts to keep equipment in working order, keeping supplies of ammunition and C-rations on hand, delivering paychecks and letters from home on time—but most fighting men took their efforts for granted. "[The man in the rear] does not realize the tremendous emotional and physical strain that men in the field are forced to endure,"[86] claimed the men of Company D.

Such was probably the case, but support personnel did not commonly live a stress-free life. Their days were often extremely long. Many worked more than twelve hours a day, six and a half days a week, an effort made more frustrating by the fact that duties sometimes seemed to have little to do with the war. "New jungle fatigues, boots, cooling fans, typewriters trickle into supply and are dispersed as needed. Also, napkins, silverware, grass seed!? Jeeze," [87] one clerk wrote home.

For some, the work was satisfying. For some it was dangerous. Stringing communication wires or taking reconnaissance (exploration) photos could mean working with dangerous equipment, making forays into the jungle, or flying into enemy airspace. For some, it was traumatizing. Henry Barber, a member of Graves Registration, was assigned to write condolence letters to families who had lost a loved one, including details of the cause of death. This regularly entailed the viewing of naked corpses, most of them grotesquely maimed and mangled. "Once we received a memo asking us to tone down the letters, to just give a vague description of the wound," he remembers. "They told us not to write 'traumatic amputation of the head' any more because it was upsetting people." [88] In order to deal with such horrors and the nightmares he began experiencing, Barber turned to alcohol and drugs.

Danger and Dancing

Even for support personnel whose work was mundane—cooks, mechanics, teletype operators, and the like—life could be rough and dangerous on smaller base camps (headquarters and resupply bases for field units) or fire bases (artillery firing positions) that were scraped out of the jungle and accessible only by helicopter. Enemy raids were common and frightening.

"Mortars do a lot of damage. The VC [Viet Cong] fire them from about five miles out, and they do it at night when they can't be seen. On the 23rd of February, my first night here, we got hit with 14 mortars about 3:30 A.M. Nobody was hurt—one helicopter was hit," [89] one former security police officer stationed at Binh Tuy writes.

Attacks by sappers (Communist commandos) could occur at any time, with the enemy storming the fences that ringed bases, cutting their way through, and screaming and laughing in attempts to de-

A mortar round explodes at an American ammunition supply depot, filling the air with shrapnel and smoke.

moralize American troops as well as destroy property and lives. "When they tried to overrun the outpost the thing that made me scaredest was having them run straight into open machinegun fire and smile, or grin, or show their teeth, and not fall," one veteran remembers. "I'd shoot 'em and shoot 'em again and they'd just stagger a little bit and keep on coming. . . . They were so screwed up on the dope and all."[90]

Men and women stationed at major bases in Saigon, Long Binh, or Cam Ranh Bay, were usually safer than soldiers on more isolated bases. A great number spent their year of service in semipeaceful surroundings, and often saw South Vietnam as an enjoyable change of scene from home. A GI who was temporarily stationed on one such base recalls, "We got to Cam Ranh in November 1968. And I got the biggest surprise of my life. There was water surfing. There was big cars being driven. There was women with fashionable clothes and men with suits on. It was not like being in a war zone. I said, Hey, what's this? Better than being home."[91]

Because they were comfortable and secure, such bases sometimes hosted well-known celebrities and entertainers who shared their talents with delighted GI audiences. One former platoon leader who had been stationed on a base at An Khe recalls, "One night, [entertainer] Lola Falana came through for a show. She was invited to a special reception, and I got to dance with her. When I called my wife on Sunday night, I said, 'Guess who I danced with?

Every Luxury

Some rear-echelon soldiers were lucky enough to be stationed at Cam Ranh Bay, one of the safest and most beautiful locales in Vietnam. There, one could escape the hardships of war, as Navy radarman Dwyte A. Brown describes in Wallace Terry's *Bloods*.

Cam Ranh Bay was the inland R & R spot. That's where the battle-weary people was supposed to come to have R & R in country. They could get everything.

And it was so beautiful, pretty country. Beautiful coral reef. And the sand. Miles of perfect white sand. And the white boys could surf all they wanted. Boy, they had their fun. . . .

I had every luxury in my room. Complete stereo with reel-to-reel tape. TV. Three-foot refrigerator full of beer and booze. Cabinets. I had a closet full of clothes. When you were on duty, you had to dress. But other times, there was no dress code. If I wanted to put a suit on one day, I wore a suit. Officers, enlisted men, be lounging around all day, like the dress code was bathing suits and sunglasses. And all the officers had a dog. I had three myself. . . .

And marijuana. Fact is I didn't even smoke marijuana 'til I went over to Vietnam. Didn't even know what marijuana was 'til I went over to Vietnam. And it was given to us. We didn't spend money in the village for it. It was a barter system. We'd bring them some steaks from the base, or a mattress. They would just give us the stuff.

I tell you I ain't even know it was a war if somebody didn't tell me. I mean I did have to be reminded sometimes there was a war going on.

Lola Falana.' And my wife said, 'I thought you were in combat.' " [92]

Black-Marketing

Despite the perks that came with some positions, many soldiers in the rear had negative feelings about life in South Vietnam. Corruption and black marketing were an ever-present state of affairs. Many South Vietnamese were quick to take advantage of the rich Americans by tempting them with jewelry, drugs, and prostitutes, sold at inflationary prices. One man wrote his friend:

> [Saigon is] almost luxurious. The MACV (Military Assistance Command/Vietnam) complex, where so many of my friends work, has a golf course, Olympic-size swimming pool, etc. But with all the surface glitter and bustle of Saigon, I came away with a very gloomy feeling. . . . The war has brought out all the venality [corruption] imaginable in these people. [93]

Eventually, many clerks and office personnel bent their principles and turned to breaking the rules and cutting deals as the quickest and most acceptable way to get things done. One former supply officer remembers:

> I traded the man from AID [Agency for International Development] a case of steaks for . . . water heaters. . . . I had gotten the steaks from some private engineering company out in the field that needed cement, and we had a whole lot of cement. The whole black market in the Army was to get what you wanted. . . . We needed a water tower, so I stole a water tower. . . . I brought in a sky crane, picked this thing up and took it over to where we were, and I have no idea who it belonged to or whatever. We needed it, so we took it. [94]

Racism

Not only did life behind the lines encourage dishonesty and corruption, it allowed meanness, pettiness, and other negative behaviors to surface. Racial discrimination was particularly apparent, despite the fact that the U.S. military had officially been de-segregated in 1948. Intolerant attitudes persisted, however, even in the field where combat veterans often insisted that racial intolerance did not exist.

Certainly, the struggle to survive drew men together and smoothed many differences in combat patrols where blacks, whites, Hispanics, and others had to rely on one another no matter what the color of their skin. Prejudice remained, though, particularly among GIs from the South, while the Black Pride movement of the late 1960s caused young black men to be less tolerant of racial slurs. Friction at times was inevitable, as one former medic notes:

> The black/white relationship was tense. I saw a couple of fist fights. It usually happened when somebody got mad, and the first thing that happens in an ar-